DEATH

of the

DEVILS'

DESTINATION

ERICA WILLIAMS

Resilient
R☯S E

P.O. Box 7295
Wesley Chapel, FL 33545
www. resilientrosewellness.com
Ordering Information:
For details, contact Erica Williams at e_williams216@yahoo.com.
The views and opinions conveyed in this book are those of the author and do not substitute for mental health treatment or professional counseling.
Scripture quotations identified NKJV, are taken from the New King James Version®.
Copyright © 1982 by Thomas Nelson. Used by permission. All rights reserved
All scripture quotations unless otherwise indicated are taken from Holy Bible, New International Version®, NIV® Copyright ©1973, 1978, 1984, 2011 by Biblica, Inc.® Used by permission. All rights reserved worldwide
Scripture quotations marked KJV are from the King James Version of Bible.

Print ISBN: 978-1-098-38528-6
eBook ISBN: 978-1-098-38529-3

Printed in the United States of America on SFI Certified paper.

First Edition

TABLE OF CONTENTS

DEDICATION

I dedicate this book to my dear mother who five years ago went home to be with our Lord Jesus Christ. If she was here today, there would be so many intricate details of my life, I would share with her. She was a woman who spoke what was on her mind and although it would sometimes hurt your feelings, she spoke truth. My prayer before the Lord called her home was to reconcile our relationship and that she accepts salvation. God granted me the desires of my heart, the day she gave her life to Christ, my husband, our children and I witnessed this momentous occasion.

I am grateful that God allowed me to immerse you in the water during your baptism and to rise again to live your new life in Christ Jesus. Also, it was an honor to be your caregiver prior to your transitioning, you held me in your arms when I took my first breath and I held you in my arms when you took your last. Mom I love and miss you more than audible words can ever express, until we see each other again, rest peacefully!

EPIGRAPH

"Adversity is an antagonist against our destiny"

FOREWORD

I have known Erica since she was a child and before. She was a happy-go-likable person, smart and mouthy. She's from a military family with three siblings, she being the oldest. As she will tell her readers, she was a "daddy's girl." At the age of eleven, her world was shattered and she was taken, by force, on a trip that would almost destroy her until she learned that where sin abounds, Grace abounds even more.

This book is a "read all" for everyone, but especially anyone who is or has experienced stepping out of the protection of the Cross. Since Erica is, by profession, a Nurse Practitioner, she mixes the spiritual diagnosis with the medical – healing for the body and spirit.

This book explains that we were made for and with a purpose from the foundations of the world, and once that purpose is interrupted, things begin to fall out of place, sort of disarrayed. But, JESUS tells us in:

1 Peter 2:29 "But you are a chosen race, a royal priesthood, a holy nation, a people for his own possession, that you may proclaim the excellencies of him who called you out of darkness into his marvelous light."

We are HIS and not of ourselves – this book tells us if we fall into separation, how to get back to HIM, as quickly as we can.

Erica completely opened up to some very personally stuff in an aid to help others find their way to Christ because of her love for others. This reminds me of Paul's ministry and what he endured because he loved JESUS and the brethren. We, as Christians should be willing to do the same.

Thank you Erica, for sharing, barring any shame, to help others find their place in this holy nation that we are a part of and to acknowledge that our citizenship is not of this world, but the Heavenly Kingdom and the requirements to live there – forever!

Laura (Pitts) Williams

PREFACE

Erica experienced much adversity as a young woman. This is why she has a love for inspiring others to pursue their God-ordained purpose with passion, poise, and perseverance. As a Nurse Practitioner and spiritual leader, Erica seeks to assist others with the tools that will unlock their hidden capabilities by way of educating, empowering, encouraging, and equipping them to live a healthy and spiritually conscious lifestyle.

Erica was inspired to write this book because of the pain she endured as a young woman while attempting to find a place of peace. The purpose of this book is to bring awareness of how the devil (enemy) will use adversity, your emotions and sin to get you off the divine destiny that God has established for your life. This book will focus on receiving a heart wound as a child, opened the door to rejection which led down a destructive path led by Erica's fragile emotions and the need to gratify her flesh to numb the pain that she was enduring.

ACKNOWLEDGMENTS

First I would like to thank God for granting me the strength, courage, and resiliency to live when I wanted to give up and die!

Second, a special thanks to my kind, compassionate, and loving husband who God created specifically for me. I cherish, honor and love him for he was the calm during my chaos, the peace in the midst of pain and the love that replaced the lust. He filled the void that I thought was incapable of being replenished.

Third I want to thank my Father Pastor Gene Lindsey, who has stood beside me and gave me wisdom even when I did not desire to hear the words he spoke. And although many times I wasn't listening, his words of wisdom and life were seeds that began to germinate after lying dormant for many years, I honor him because he made me into the woman you see today.

Next I want to thank my four beautiful children that gave me a reason to live, set goals, and pursue my ambitions. They are my gifts from God that has brought me much joy.

INTRODUCTION

I never imagined myself writing a book. It was spoken to me three separate times that I would write books; however, at the time these words seemed insignificant and surreal for I was unable to see spiritually the plan and purpose God had for my life. I can recall the first time this word was spoken over my life—it was the year 2010. This word was spoken over my life two additional times in the year 2016. Not until God spoke this to me on July 22, 2016, though, did the previously spoken words become real. They became so real I could see in the spirit as God was speaking. Right in front of my very own eyes, I immediately could see the actual words as He spoke, and the title and the front cover of this book.

I knew the dream I had of becoming an author was possible because I was seeing the manifestations through His eternal eyes and not my limited carnal eyesight. At that very moment, my spiritual eyesight and the wisdom of the Holy Spirit became unlocked and readily available unto me. It was as if a locked door had suddenly flung open and I could access everything God has for me. In order to access the promises of God, you must follow His established course!

I was inspired to write this book because of the love I have for women who have been abused, abandoned, and broken as a result. I discovered that in order to be made whole again, I had to travel back to a place in time that was familiar yet painful, hurtful yet healing, and forgotten but yet kept me bound. The Holy Spirit revealing to me the archived pain brought forth much-needed freedom. I had to recover the fragmented pieces of my life left in many different places and with various people.

As I traveled down memory lane, it opened up hidden, deep, dark secrets I knew not of and memories that were once suppressed begin to manifest. Overwhelming emotions of anger, bitterness, hate, low self-esteem, and rejection begin to reappear. The door to these emotions had to be reopened and properly closed in order for me to heal completely. During your time of reading this book, I will bring awareness of how the enemy will use adversity, emotions, and sin to get you off the divine destiny God has established for your life. This book will focus on how my receiving a heart wound as a child opened the door to rejection that led me down a destructive path following my emotions and the need to gratify my flesh to numb the pain I was enduring. You do not have to allow the decisions and circumstances of others to dictate the final outcome of your life as I did. I ask you to climb into this vehicle, buckle your seatbelt, and enjoy the ride with me on a journey into my life but your destiny!

POEM

Creation

All of My creation knows its place.

They make haste to stay in their space.

Not leaving their borders unless they hear My cry,

Never, not once, asking Me why.

The Moon obeys and changes places with the Sun.

The Sun obeys and shines for the sustainment of mankind.

The trees obey, for they sway to provide O2 each and every day.

The rain obeys and knows to fall, to provide water for all.

The wind obeys and knows when to blow, to prevent my people from being tossed to and fro.

The oceans and seas listen to my word so that they don't overflow into my land.

All of creation made by My hands hears My voice and obey My plans, except **MAN!!!**

CHAPTER 1

Deception

Being forced to live a lie that began when I was only eleven years old took a toll on my life as I entered adulthood. This lie caused me so much pain that I began believing this was normal. The intensity of this pain lured me to seek out enjoyment that would numb the pain and appease my flesh. These sensual pleasures were divisive and divertive, for they took me down a path of darkness uninhabited by God. That dark path took many twists and turns almost to the point of no return. Along this journey I was trapped in a body I hated and misunderstood.

I was blind to the fact that I was created in the image and likeness of God, and I knew not my worth. My distorted views of myself were of someone who was unworthy, unproductive, and unessential. I was a wounded soul walking around with a fragmented heart, yet I had no knowledge of this. When an individual is wounded he/she is incapable of operating fully in his or her God-ordained capacity, thereby rendering him/her ineffective to set free that which is held captive. Not only was my spirit wounded, but my heart was wounded and fragmented, comparable to a glass shattered into millions of pieces.

During this time my soul was restless and agitated. I was living in a place of stagnation and contemplation. The stagnation kept me attached to tightened shackles so that I could not move forward in my life, and the contemplation had me contemplating ending my futile life. I was unable to reproduce or receive the love of God from a place of reality. I was oblivious to establishing boundaries in my life underpinned by biblical principles. These multitudinous heart wounds blinded my physical and spiritual vision and my thought processes become obscured (concealed, hidden, and masked).

An old cliché warns "your perception is your reality," but I will say this is not true because our perception at times can become distorted. You may ask what distorts our perception. Our beliefs, desires, emotions, habits, and thoughts, seeking to gratify and appease the flesh, will cause our perception to become distorted! These misperceptions can take the form of adultery, alcohol, drug addictions, deceit, familiar spirits, fornication, idolatry, sex addictions, perversion, lies, manipulations, ungodly relationships, thoughts, habits, rituals, and routines. The enemy will utilize our misperceptions to beguile and ensnare us. Once our thoughts become distorted or if we allow the enemy to pervert them, we run the risk of getting off the course God has predestined for us.

When we begin to believe or yield to our distorted perceptions over God's divine plan we begin to make wrong choices in our lives and become acquainted with people who do not have our best interests at heart. Once this occurs we begin to take detours off the path on which God has placed us, or we attempt to take a shortcut. We begin to think our way is the right way, we become analytical in our thought processes, and often we forget to involve God in our daily lives and decision-making. However, we must know we will never be as intelligent as God, and a successful life is inevitable only if we to seek God, for He is the creator and we are the created.

You may ask, how do I seek God? Ways of seeking God include reading His holy word (the Bible), prayer, worship, and praising Him for who He is, the Savior, the Lamb slain before the foundations of the world. Praying is our way of communicating with God daily, actively listening to Him, and obeying His instructions. We worship Him by studying His holy word (the Bible) and desiring a close and intimate relationship with Him, setting time aside out of our busy lives to seek Him.

Just as when you purchase a product and inside the packaging is a manual that gives complete details on the proper operation of that product, God being our creator and the author of our lives has the instructions for how we should live and operate on earth.

Isaiah 55:8–9 New King James Version (NKJV): 8 "For My thoughts are not your thoughts, nor are your ways My ways," says the Lord. 9 "For as the heavens are higher than the earth, so are My ways higher than your ways and My thoughts than your thoughts."

As the created, we must seek God (the creator) for His wisdom, knowledge, and understanding on how to live this thing called life, what path we should choose, and how to operate this fleshly vehicle in order to reach our God-ordained destiny. We can choose to take many paths and detours in life such as excitement, lust, greed, fornication, addictions, and perversion. This list is not exhaustive.

Psalms 119:105 (NKJV) declares: Your word is a lamp to my feet And a light to my path.

We must know that once we have chosen these paths, if we have not sought God concerning the encounters we may face along the journey, we will find ourselves open to the wilderness, attacked by the enemy, and in a dark, defeated state. God has chosen a path for all our lives; however, in our own carnal wisdom, at the direction/discretion of others, or because we want to fit in and be validated by others, we choose the path that suits our fleshly desires or the desires of those we have relationships with. This is how my tempestuous journey began, seeking to please my flesh but unaware of the pain, distorted perception, and heart wounds that would challenge and oppose my purpose.

Destiny

Oh, Destiny, Destiny, where could you be?

Hidden under a rock or in a tree?

I've searched the shore, sand, and sea

Only to find you're too far from me.

My mind is blinded from many who speak

Words of death, bondage, and unreality.

I appear to be fine exteriorly,

Although with each beat of my heart, I profusely bleed.

For my heart is broken, why can't you see?

Oh, now I know, for you did it to me!

CHAPTER 2

Having a Blast But on a Troubled Path

Once upon a time I got into my car. I backed out of the driveway of my Father's house and began to drive. I did not realize that along for the journey had come an invisible passenger (Satan), who I became so comfortable with that when he asked for the keys, I gave them to him willingly and without a fight. So, of course, he began to drive and the trip was much longer than I expected. In the beginning I was having so much fun and my fleshly desires were being fulfilled so completely that I forgot the directions back to my Father's house.

Before I could realize or comprehend what was taking place, my invisible driver had turned down a street called Pleasure that ran into Lustful Junction. Next we traveled onto Fornication Highway; we made a couple of stops at Good Sex Gas Station to fill up along the way. After we filled up our journey resumed until we detoured and had a layover at House of Hell Marriage. House of Hell Marriage was intriguing at first because I thought I could live there forever off love and happiness, only to find it was furnished with deceit, hatred, lies, manipulation, sleeping around, putdowns, and beat downs. Finally I broke free and escaped the abuse, pain, and torment of House of Hell Marriage, but not without a price. The price I paid was the happiness, stability, and security of my children. I received in return unhealed, infected physical, and psychological wounds, scars, and shadows.

After leaving House of Hell Marriage we approached a dark, winding road called Depression, but along the way we turned onto Low Self-Esteem Road, Suicidal Court, Prideful Drive, and then Destruction Boulevard, which turned into Death Cul-de-sac, which appeared to be a dead end! However, my Father, whose house I had left what seemed like so long ago, came and rescued me for I forgot some of the most valuable lessons He had taught me. Allow me to share them with you as I invite you into my troubled past, although I thought I was having a blast!

Pay attention as I share my life, my story, and the aftermath. I can remember my life being turned upside down when I was at the tender, innocent age of eleven—my parents divorced. The life I once knew began to transform into a life of unfamiliarity. I say this because to go from being in a home with both parents to being in a home with just one parent (my mother) was out of the ordinary and unimaginable. I was very comfortable and complete with my family living under one roof. I am the oldest out of my siblings and the only daughter, so of course, I was a daddy's girl to the core. Not seeing my daddy before I went to bed and when I awakened in the morning was torture to my eleven-year-old mind. And although I could not fully process or rationalize these feelings, I felt as if a death had occurred. Confusion and anger set in, and the joyful illuminating child I once was began to transform into something cold and dark.

Prior to these life changing events, I was vibrant and I loved to entertain my family with singing. I enjoyed singing and entertaining; my desire was to become a recording artist. My grandmother gave me the nickname Blackbird because I loved to sing. But soon after my parents divorced, my singing ceased. I no longer desired to sing anything, and my beautiful voice became silenced. This Blackbird felt like a caged bird without bars, shattered without proof of the scars, so I thought! Quickly I begin to realize that this new living arrangement wasn't working out in my best interest.

I went from living in a loving, stable home to being gripped by the jaws and teeth of the projects. This was another area of unfamiliarity. I was not used to seeing drug addicts and people hanging outside all times of the night, hearing people hollering sexual innuendoes at me, being bullied on the school bus, and picked on because of how I dressed and talked. To add insult to injury, I was exposed to strange people coming to our home to play cards and not being able to sleep at night for the loud noise and commotion that took place downstairs. My bedroom was my ark of safety. I would sit in my room for hours imagining how my life would be if my family still lived together. My childhood imagination was intensely vivid, and it remains so now that I am an adult. I would listen to music, without the desire to sing, but my vivid imagination and the music seemed to calm my troubled thoughts and feelings of abandonment.

Meanwhile, these card games became quite frequent, taking place pretty much every weekend. The card playing caused further chaos in my life. These card games were a game changer in my life, for one night, during one of these card games, I was raped at the age of fourteen in my very own bed and exposed to the enemy's second plot to destroy my future. I don't know if I understood what the term *rape* meant at the time of this violation. *Rape* is defined as unlawful sexual activity involving sexual intercourse by force or under the threat of harm. The person who raped me entered my room, held me down with his hand over my mouth, and forced his penis inside of me. He was much older than me and stronger; therefore, I did not have the strength to fight back for I was a child being taken advantage of by an adult male who shattered my innocence, infiltrated my purity, and stole my virginity.

After this sexual assault the feelings of violation were overwhelming. I was devastated and unable to comprehend what had just taken place! There I was lying in my bed, weeping, attempting to process what had just happened, and feeling like a piece of trash that needed to be disposed of. Additionally, the pain I felt on the inside of my vagina was quite traumatic for it was swollen on the outside and throbbing with pain. Upon my going to the bathroom, as I sat down on the toilet and pulled my panties down to my knocking knees, I noticed a large amount of bright red blood that covered the seat of my peach-colored underwear, which, by the way, was my favorite pair. I had to hide my underwear until I was able to throw it away for fear I had done something wrong. Being raped in the comfort of my bed made me feel nasty, unworthy, hopeless, shameful, and fearful to even sleep in the place I had thought was my shelter from harm and danger. As my adult mind travels back to this place, I now know my innocence was stolen for I was a virgin violated in my home, which should have been free from thieves and wolves.

My room went from my sanctuary to a prison of dark memories and motives. This person would come in my room and rape me every time he came over to play cards. This act became the norm for me and I grew numb and immune to the inner pain, so much so that I begin enjoying the sexual encounters. When my mother would go to bed I would leave the back door unlocked so he could come in and have his way with me. Enjoying these sexual escapades was me manifesting Stockholm syndrome. Webster-Merriam defines *Stockholm syndrome* as a condition in which a hostage develops a psychological alliance with his/her captors during captivity. During the sexual encounters I developed an emotional bond and felt I was in love with this man who threatened my family's lives and stole my most prized possessions, my vagina and my identity. This was an irrational belief that the enemy diabolically plotted to destroy my destiny.

During this time an older man was teaching me perverted sexual acts, even though I was a child who knew nothing about the long-term scars they would leave buried in my mind and heart! The enemy was utilizing manipulation, hormones, and emotions to captivate and enslave me. Sex began to be a tool I could utilize to mask my pain. My immature mind was being manipulated by the invisible enemy and the sex hormones the body produces during sexual intercourse. And my body was enjoying the stimulation of the two working together to pervert my purpose and conceal my identity.

The stimulation of my mind and body under the spell of a chemical cocktail of cortisol, dopamine, testosterone, adrenaline, phenethylamine, endorphins, and oxytocin gave me an unexplainable excitement. Let's just say I became addicted to sex as a crack user is to crack. Although the high was temporary and after each sexual encounter I would find myself depressed and ashamed, it did not change the fact that I wanted to repeat the cycle not only with the man who initially raped me but with other men as well. It was as if I had to have sex to survive. I was utilizing sex as a survival mechanism while opening the door of my heart to fragmentation and ungodly soul ties.

Repetition is the process of doing a particular thing that has already been done before. I compare repetition to a merry-go-round. It goes around and around in the same direction, unable to divert to another direction. And by chance if you stay on a merry-go-round long enough, it causes you to become dizzy and disoriented. Both of those combinations will cause you to stumble and fall once you decide to get off this circular cycle. The enemy utilizes repetitive negative sinful cycles to ensnare us, and once we are ensnared by these cycles they become strongholds designed to keep you stagnant or in a falling state, disabling you from reaching your full potential in who God created you to become. The massive yet insidious changes that took place in my life—from my parents' divorce, to rape, to becoming a sex addict—was enough to shatter the most fortified heart.

Being raped is comparable to being robbed; a possession has been taken away from you against your will. Furthermore, the initial incident of this rape was rehearsed over and over (repetitively) in my mind with each replay leaving behind deeply rooted unexplainable pain. This pain transitioned into depression, so much so that I began having suicidal ideations. I was experiencing post-traumatic stress disorder (PTSD), defined as a common anxiety disorder that develops after exposure to a terrifying event or ordeal in which grave physical harm occurred or was threatened. After being raped, victims are left with psychological scars and they oftentimes suffer in silence because of guilt, shame, and fear. Those three words—*guilt, shame,* and *fear*—gripped me like a coat on a cold winter day.

I began to suffer from depression, low self-esteem, and rejection. I felt that no one else in my life cared, so why should I? Rape can cause tremendous distress in the victim's life, especially if they are unable to share the event and their emotions with someone they can trust. Due to this hidden secret, which no one knew of except God, my predator, and me, my life spiraled out of control. I was unable to share this event with my parents for fear of them blaming me and of my rapist harming my family. The inability to give my pain a voice resulted in me becoming attached to the trauma. Many years went by with all of these private proclivities etched within my heart.

Addictions

Multiple addictions call my name.

Lust, sex, food, drugs, and alcohol—they all play the game.

Indulging in them all to numb the pain,

No sense of boundaries and, yes, I have no shame.

Right or wrong, rejected and disrespected,

There's no shield to keep my heart protected.

Shattered into thousands of pieces,

Oh, Lord, this is more than I expected.

Craving them again, but I can't and won't neglect it!

CHAPTER 3

Shattered Heart

The physical heart was created to sustain life. The heart consists of four chambers that each have a unique, different function. The right atrium receives blood from the veins and pumps it to the right ventricle. The right ventricle receives blood from the right atrium and pumps it to the lungs, where it is loaded with oxygen. The left atrium receives oxygenated blood from the lungs and pumps it to the left ventricle. The left ventricle (the strongest chamber) pumps oxygen-rich blood to the rest of the body.

The heart's essential function is to pump blood to the entire body. The blood has life in it, for if the heart fails to do its job, then the body dies due to the deprivation of oxygen. I know you may be wondering why I am giving an anatomy class. I'm glad you asked this important question. Let's begin to connect the dots. Spiritually our hearts must be guarded from infiltration of burdens created as a result of trauma. Merriam-Webster defines *trauma* as a psychological or behavioral disorder resulting from severe mental or emotional stress. The state of not receiving oxygen is called *anoxia* and a lack of or decreased oxygen is *hypoxia*. If the body does not have proper oxygen distribution, it begins to malfunction and death ensues if there's no intervention.

Proverbs 4:23 (NIV): 23 Above all else, guard your heart, for everything you do flows from it.

Likewise, with our spiritual heart, if we allow it to become corrupt, contaminated, and infiltrated with ungodly habits and desires, it causes us to function improperly. The path to our destiny becomes obscured and instead of being an illuminating vessel on the earth we become despondent, desolate, and destitute. Basically, our spiritual walk ceases and our growth and development are insidiously halted. Just as physical flowers, plants, and trees cannot grow without sunlight, we cannot grow or develop without the Son of God. If no intervention is sought, we begin to die spiritually and our destiny is surely doomed.

When our hearts are wounded we are unable to operate in a healthy state in our daily lives and within the body of Christ. We become a tainted or toxic vessel while attempting to do His will. Anything that's toxic is venomous and does not stay confined to its point of origination but continues to spread to the surrounding areas, thereby contaminating anything in its path. I became very toxic and began destroying anything in my path. My thoughts, intentions, emotions, and desires were malignant.

The malignancy began to transform the very existence of who God created me to be into a darkened state. How could this be, you may ask, being that God's word annotates that we were created in God's image and likeness? This is the enemy's goal: to change the very identity and trajectory of your life. He does this hoping you won't reproduce and replicate God on the earth. Not only will you not replicate God in the Earth, this malignancy strangles the life out of your responsibilities as daughters, mothers, wives, sisters, aunts, and friends. If allowed, heart wounds have the ability to complicate and destroy much-needed relationships with God and those you love.

Eventually I realized I was unable to love God, others, and myself because my heart was severely fragmented. When your heart is shattered into pieces, it becomes fragmented and a piece of who you are is left in the time and space in which the traumatic experience occurred. You become unbalanced, unequal, and unstable. You are no longer whole in your spirit, soul, and body. Often the memories of the actual event are suppressed, which is a survival mechanism. If we could recall every traumatic experience that has occurred in our lives, we would become so overwhelmed with anger, anxiety, fear, hurt, depression, and pain, that our psyche could not handle it and as a result we would have a nervous breakdown.

Heart wounds are demonic in nature because they affect every aspect of an individual's life: spirit, soul, and body. When a person's heart is wounded, if they don't receive the proper treatment, other abnormalities and infirmities will occur. Not receiving an intervention will cause surreptitious spiritual and/or physical death. Heart wounds are traumatic experiences that we may have acquired during our childhood years. Over time these wounds become repressed and hidden and begin taking root within our hearts. If allowed, the root will poison our souls, thereby producing distorted beliefs, behaviors, and patterns that originate in the soulish realm. Once this occurs, we become bound to dysfunctional thought patterns (soulish/carnal) that manifest as fear, anxiety, depression, anger, conflict, confusion, guilt, shame, rejection, and unforgiveness.

In the previous paragraph I mentioned the term *patterns*; the enemy is divisive when it comes to utilizing patterns precisely to destroy purpose. His plan is to separate you from demonstrating God's image and to divert you from the road God ordained to establish your purpose. His desire is to pervert your true identity. God has a set order for mankind and how everything should bear fruit according to its original seed. This multiplication produces glorification of God as the creator. God's order is always that of holiness and righteousness, two attributes He possess. As the created being, we must reproduce God on the earth in all walks of life. Satan's plan is to pervert and divert. But God's plan is to convert and propel—to convert us into the image of Jesus Christ, which propels us into our true identity and purpose.

A purported identity causes many of us to walk around portraying an image that is camouflaged because we do not desire for others to know that we are angry, broken, defeated, depressed, hurting, and resentful. We harbor shame, unforgiveness, and weakness due to wounds of times past caused by another, possibly someone we loved, trusted, and respected. Wounds manifest in the form of abuse, whether it be physical, psychological, sexual, spiritual, or verbal. Portraying a false identity is easy when no one can see the well-hidden invisible scars.

The wound may have occurred during the critical years of your development when your personality was evolving. A wound to our soul is an injury to our spiritual being that has occurred in the emotions, mind, and will. These wounds are not visible to the naked eye; however, to the spiritual eye they are, for they scream out to those who can see spiritually as an ambulance siren blaring as it transports a critically ill patient to the emergency room. When the soul is wounded we exhibit characteristics contrary to being created in God's image and likeness.

We display behaviors that are out of order with the word of God and unpleasing to Him.

Proverbs 15:13 (KJV): A merry heart maketh a cheerful countenance but by sorrow of the heart the spirit is broken.

The soul has four compartments just as the heart does: mind (thoughts), will (our ambitions), emotions (our feelings), and conscience (our moral guide). The soul is what makes up an individual's personality, the innate nature of mankind. The soul or mind is the vehicle that nourishes our reasoning, pleasures, affections, thoughts, passions, desires, appetites, ambitions, endeavors, and purposes. If we allow the four compartments to become contaminated or infiltrated with the enemy's enticing words, those words defile those compartments within us. When we entertain negative thoughts, we grant them permission to grow. What causes the heart to become wicked and defiled by our thoughts and intentions? Allowing the negative, wicked, and evil thoughts Satan brings to our minds to be played out and displayed in our daily lives and atmosphere.

The enemy is very subtle, and he uses deception to gain dominion within our lives. When he speaks to your mind, it's in the first person, therefore we, being unaware of this deception, carry out his will under the false pretense of thinking it's our individual thoughts and decisions. If we do not cast them down, they have the potential to take root in our hearts. Once this root begins to grow, it will affect and/or infect different areas of our lives, including our relationships with others as aunts, daughters, sisters, wives, mothers, friends, and coworkers. The invisible enemy, the devil, wants to destroy your atmosphere by any means necessary, and he will utilize another human being to carry out his manipulative mission.

1 Peter 5:8 (NKJV): 8 Be sober, be vigilant because your adversary the devil walks about like a roaring lion, seeking whom he may devour.

Heart wounds have the capability of hiding the true identity of an individual as the individual will live out his/her life and interact with those around him/her from a place of hurt and pain from the past. What disrupts our true identity are: past emotional wounds and unhealed scars caused by people who have been hurt themselves; it's a repetitive cycle. Hurt people vandalize others! If we do not allow the Holy Spirit to heal us, this grants the enemy a legal right to wreak havoc in our daily lives, thereby destroying our identity, relationships, and divine purpose. Once purpose is destroyed, our authority and kingdom dominion become dormant. God gave mankind dominion so we could establish order within our homes, relationships, and the territory in which we live.

Traumatic experiences occurring during the critical years of personality development can and will cause an individual to stagnate in their psychosocial development, which begins during the childhood years. Disruptions occurring during the developmental stage of a child's life can cause negative outcomes. Erik Erikson, a developmental psychologist and psychoanalyst, advocated that personality development is manifested through eight stages from infancy to the geriatric years. He believed an identity crisis results from a painful event that surfaced during the adolescent years; this identity crisis could have either a negative or a positive outcome for ego and personality development. According to Saul McLeod, "For Erikson (1958, 1963), these crises are of a psychosocial nature because they involve psychological needs of the individual (i.e., psycho) conflicting with the needs of society (i.e., social)." "According to the theory, successful completion of each stage results in a healthy personality and the acquisition of basic virtues. Basic virtues are characteristic strengths which the ego can use to resolve subsequent crises."

The stage in which my traumatic event occurred was that of Erikson's stage five: Identity vs. Role Confusion. In this stage the adolescent (twelve to eighteen years old) begins seeking for who he or she is (personal identity) by way of instilled personal values, beliefs, and goals. My being raped caused an identity crisis in which I became confused and harrowed with unanswered questions in the form of who, what, when, and where. *Who am I? What is my purpose? When does my role as an adult begin? Where do I belong as a young female in society?* Through much prayer and seeking God, I have come to discover that I was stuck in a time capsule. Although I looked on the exterior like a young adult, my thought process was that of an eleven-year-old little girl crying out for help in the form of anger. Arrested development was in full operation within my psyche. *Arrested development* is a medical term that describes a chronic medical disorder or disability with an onset in childhood where development has stopped prematurely. Spiritual arrested development is designed to stop, slow, seize, and capture the soul of an emotionally and physically immature person, thereby keeping them a hostage to stagnation and producing ineffectiveness, powerlessness, and hopelessness in carrying out the will of God for his/her life. Ultimately the enemy imprisons the individual in hopes of that person never achieving the plans and purpose God ordained for his/her life before birth.

The heart is the mind, will, and emotions—it is the seat, the center of the soul. When an individual is wounded in the heart, the wound compromises the body (physically and spiritually). Earlier I discussed that blood has life infused within it. Speaking from a spiritual aspect, the blood within our hearts yields life to the seeds that have been planted via negative or positive experiences, and eventually a harvest will manifest. The harvest that manifested in my life was immaturity, instability, and immorality. I made erratic, life-altering decisions based off of my tainted emotions. The decisions I made were coming from an impure, wounded heart that sought to hurt myself and others within my path, although psychologically I was unaware.

As a result, I wandered around aimlessly trying to put together the missing pieces and during the process I became anxious, frustrated, and impatient. I began to feel terribly overwhelmed, tormented in my mind, depressed, and utterly defeated. Fear began to grip my inner being, and I thought to myself, "there's no way I'm escaping this place." That fear transitioned into rejection. I begin rejecting myself and in my mind I felt that others rejected me because of my history. Self-rejection played a major role in my not understanding my true identity. My identity was obscured; my facial recognition was that of Erica, but my heart revealed brokenness. Brokenness can present itself in different facets of our lives. My identity at that time in my life did not bear witness to who God created me to be. Brokenness will open the door to personality disorders and a person will begin to exhibit different personalities with the different people they encounter just to be accepted under false pretenses. I latched onto this unhealthy survival mechanism because I did not want to face my issues.

As women we wear multiple hats, but we have one heart that can become overwhelmed and stressed with the cares and the burdens of everyday life. And for some of us who are or who have been single parents, this intensifies until we begin to feel overwhelmed, heavy, depressed, unloved, unappreciated, and unwanted, and we begin doubting who we are. Not only do we begin to doubt who we are, we question ourselves as to where we fit into the puzzle of this thing called life. Once all these things plague our minds, we begin to question God and dismiss the plan He has for us. We lose sight of His vision and promises and of path He ordained for us before the foundation of the world. Unbeknownst to me at the time, God will allow us to continue on our troubled path until we reach a place where we can be processed anew. Although opposition comes to knock us out of position, adversity processes us into the next chapter of our life, a new beginning fueled with empowerment and purpose.

During your time of reading this book if you have discovered your heart has been wounded, please say the prayer on the next page out loud. As you pray, allow the Holy Spirit to totally heal those areas that plague your thoughts and keep you bound to past events. The Holy Spirit is your teacher and comforter. He's patient, he understands your pain, and he will walk you through the process of freedom.

Special Note: Remember it is the Holy Spirit that grants us the ability to forgive others who have hurt, abused, deceived, and rejected us. We cannot forgive within ourselves—the flesh does not have the capability to do this—but the spirit of men and women can forgive by yielding to the voice and instructions of the Holy Spirit.

PRAYER OF FREEDOM FROM HEART WOUNDS

Heavenly Father, I come before your throne of grace and mercy, asking that you forgive me for allowing this heart wound to hinder your purpose and will for my life. Father, I ask that you forgive my offender/s_____ (Names) _____ and I ask, Father, that you would cleanse me and them from all unrighteousness. Father, I thank you that your blood purchased my salvation, healing, and deliverance. My desire is to apply your shed blood to the past hurts, pains, and scars that torment my body, soul, and spirit. Father, I know Jesus was wounded for my transgressions, the chastisement of my peace was upon him, and by His stripes I am healed and whole in mind, body, and spirit. Father, I thank you for your perpetual love that renders healing. I receive your unfailing eternal love and the Holy Spirit's comfort and truth concerning the areas that were held captive in my life. As I listen to the voice of the Holy Spirit, I will replace every lie I've accepted with the truth of your words concerning my life. I renounce and break covenant with sin, iniquity, transgression every word of death, desolation, and destruction that was spoken over my life. I repent of allowing the enemy and others to distract me from the purpose for which you created me. I thank you Father for restoring me back to my rightfully place. Now that I have received my healing, I thank you that you allow me to see spiritually the wounds of others so that I can offer the bread of life and living water to others. I thank you for releasing me from bondage and utilizing me to bring your name glory and for granting me the authority to set the captives free in Jesus's name. Amen!

Process

My thoughts are stuck in an unprecedented place called space
and time.

Beep, Beep, I hear the clock chime.

Now the hour has come to choose my path.

How can I,

When I continue to indulge in the aftermath?

I hear His voice calling, it's time for your next.

So many choices—they all seem so complex.

But I must trust the process and take the initial step!

CHAPTER 4

Perception

God's word in Proverbs 14:12 (AMP) states, "There is a way which seems right to a man and appears straight before him, but at the end of it is the way of death."

Here God is saying your way may seem right, may sound right, may look right, may smell right, and may even taste right, but your perception is limited. The key word is *your* because what may seem real or factual to you to others is not. The enemy will utilize what YOU PERCEIVE to manipulate and deceive you!!! However, perception in the eyes of Jesus is the only reality. We must see things through His eyes and not our own for our vision is very limited, even more so when we are in sin. Merriam-Webster defines *perception* as the process of recognizing and interpreting sensory stimuli (e.g., someone touching your arm). What is *sensory*? *Sensory* is the ability to sense pleasure. Sensory receptors are located on the dermis and epidermis of the skin. They have the capability to respond to external and internal stimuli and to relay this information to the brain, where it is interpreted.

We know that we have five senses: sight, hearing, smell, taste, and touch. However, research has proven human beings have nine senses altogether. The other four are thermoception, nociception, equilibrioception, and proprioception. *Thermoception* is the sense of heat and the absence of heat (cold) by way of internal skin passages. *Nociception* is the nonconscious perception of nerve damage or damage to tissue; it's the ability to sense or feel (pain). *Equilibrioception* is the perception of balance or acceleration and can be altered when fluid is in the inner ear. *Proprioception* is the perception of bodily awareness as it relates to space and movement (the term derives from the Latin word *proprius*, meaning "one's own, individual"). If I close my eyes and someone raises my hand above my head, I should be able to sense the position of my hand.

The reason I say our perception is limited is because when adversity is headed our way, we are unable to discern it because as human beings, our perception is limited by what we see, hear, smell, taste, and touch. We get caught up in our feelings and emotions, which I call "falsification of the fleshly nature." How many know your flesh will fool you and lead you down a path to destruction onto a dead-end route leading to death, if you allow yourself to yield to it? The flesh seeks gratification and that gratification leads us down a road called sin. And if you're not familiar with the results of sin, let me say this— it will lead you astray, keep you longer than you anticipated to stay, and cost you what you can't afford or aren't willing to pay! I say this because I was in this state. I thought my way was right and it took me down a path of destruction until the point of death! My distorted perception manifested when I was eleven and continued well into my adulthood.

These sexual encounters continued until my mother found out, which led to her pressing charges against the man and me being imprisoned in my own home. The only places I was allowed to go were school, my grandmother's house, and weekend visits with my father. Although my mother uncovered my shameful secret, I did not share with her that this man had raped me until I was well into my thirties. After the sexual encounters ended with this man, I begin craving sex, not realizing the craving was a cry for help and love. My teenage years were filled with so much pain I found myself in a rebellious state, not caring about myself or how others felt or thought of me.

This rebellious state caused a strain on my relationship with my mother, and I know now I blamed her for the divorce and my being sadistically raped. My rebellious state caused me to run away from home. At the age of sixteen on a hawkish, cold Friday night, I left home. I stayed gone from home about three days, which seemed more like thirty. I walked the streets at night not being afraid or caring about what could or would happen to me. You've heard the cliché that "God takes care of babies and fools," and I must say I can attest to this because I was foolishly out of my mind walking the streets at night by myself. Looking back at this time frame within my life, I could have been raped a second time or even worse, murdered.

My being murdered would have caused overwhelming grief and distress for my parents. Indeed my premature death would have robbed me a second time. I would have been robbed of God's purpose He created me to fulfill on the earth. My parents would have been robbed of spending time with me and watching me grow into womanhood, and they would have never gotten the chance to spend time with their four beautiful grandchildren, who now are all grown! Hallelujah; God had His hand upon my life and future!

While on a temporary unauthorized vacation from home, I walked ten miles to the home of a young man I dated, and he allowed me to stay with him in his bedroom unbeknownst to his mother. Monday morning arrived, and it was time for us both to go to school. His mother came into the room to wake him up for school and found me lying peacefully beside him. I say peacefully because being in his presence made me forget about the torment, confusion, and chaotic mess taking place inside my mind and body. To make a long story short, his mother woke both of us up from our blissful sleep, and she was not happy to have an uninvited stranger lying in bed with her one and only son. Needless to say, neither of us went to school that day. She lectured the two of us and called my parents.

My mother and grandmother came and picked me up. Initially they seemed genuinely happy to see me, but following the cheers of joy were the curse words and accusations. I was accused of being on drugs. I was called crazy, a slut, a b--ch, and a whore. I was told I wouldn't be sh-t in life and that if I had gotten pregnant, I would be on my own. I was called various filthy names, every name but child of God. My mother told me I was no longer welcome to live with her and my siblings, which didn't seem so bad because I wanted to break free from house arrest.

After leaving my boyfriend's home, while sitting in the backseat listening to them defame my character, I felt numb and immune to their merciless insults. My mother, extremely angry, turned around and punched me a couple of times in my face. At that point I cared nothing about what my mother thought of me for I blamed her for the torment and immense pain that consumed me. Furthermore, to add insult to injury, they took me to the local hospital emergency room to have me checked for drug usage and committed to the behavioral health unit. Once I had been released from the emergency room, my father took me home. He explained to me how much pain I had caused everyone and that I was going to be punished. To know my father is to understand that he, a man of much wisdom, can talk to you and make you feel immensely regretful and not want to commit the incident ever again. What came after the talk was very shocking. He told me to prepare for a whipping. I was shocked because my father had never whipped me before and here I was at sixteen years old getting my first whipping from him.

My preparation for the spanking consisted of me putting on three pairs of sweatpants for fear of the unknown. Patiently, with much love in his voice, my father told me to go take off the sweatpants and put on some shorts. Right about then I was shaking like a leaf on a tree during a breezy day. Humbly, I obeyed his orders and he, dressed in his army battle dress uniform, expressed to me loudly that he did not come to talk but was ready for battle. I can recall my heart rate accelerating to the point that I thought it was going to hop right out of my chest. While my father was putting a leather belt to my behind, he was talking to me and crying all at the same time. I knew by his actions that I had caused him devastating hurt and pain. Until this day I regret the pain I caused both of my parents for they did not deserve this. I was acting out because of the pain I was feeling from their divorce and the rape.

Once the eventful weekend was over and I returned to school, I became deeply depressed and ashamed of how I had behaved. My new living arrangements, which I did not care for, were with my father and his wife. The stress of this transition caused me to not care about my assignments. My grades begin to decline; I went from excelling in school to barely doing enough to get by. My parents were concerned about my safety, and because I was so distracted by the pain, bitterness, and sexual cravings I did not stop to think how I was affecting those who loved me. At the time my concern was that I would no longer allow my mother to treat me like a prisoner. I wanted to break free and to do what I perceived was right in my distorted, immature mind. The term *freedom* was foreign to me because my mind was occupied by multiple distractions.

Freedom is a term used to denote the liberty to express who you are in the way you carry yourself, dress, speak, and interact with others. Due to the past hurts, disappointments, and rape, I was not free but enslaved to my past. The overwhelming pain I felt caused me to be ensnared by my flesh. When my flesh spoke, I obeyed its every command, not realizing what it would cost me. Insurmountable internal stressors plagued my thought process, paralyzing my ability to comprehend the reality of life. Those internal stressors were abandonment, guilt, shame, rejection, bitterness, anger, torment, unforgiveness, hurt, and pain.

Many of our internal stressors are based on delusions and lies. These delusions and lies are more acceptable than God's truth of who we are in Him. We have been fed lies from the enemy and sometimes from those we trust. We have a false sense of reality related to the world and the way we should navigate through life. As a result, our interactions with others are expressed as unreality. The true identity of the person is hidden and that which you see is of darkness.

We must come to understand that there's no growth in darkness. If the sun refused to shine, all life as we know it would cease to exist. Likewise, if we allow our internal stressors to continue, the result is a spiritual death (an unfruitful, unproductive life). Although the internal stressors I endured were the result of past incidents, I did not have to allow the residue of those stressors to perpetuate. Allowing our internal stressors to dominate our daily lives only enslaves us and places us in bondage, which brings along its friends chaos, doubt, sin, and a disconnection from Jesus (light). Disconnection is a result of being more focused on those things than we are on God. It is the light that promotes growth, restoration, and regeneration.

John 8:12 (NKJV): Then Jesus spoke to them again, saying, "I am the light of the world. He who follows Me shall not walk in darkness, but have the light of life."

The divorce of my parents was a doorway that led to my initial hurt. I was very distraught and immensely saddened by my parents' divorce, which allowed another door to be opened to abandonment. At the time in my life I did not understand these terms, but I do remember my mother saying often that our father had abandoned us. What are doorways, you may ask. Let me see if I can explain the analogy. We all know what a physical door looks like.

The textbook definition defines *door* as a hinged or otherwise movable barrier that allows ingress and egress into an "enclosure." The opening in the wall can be referred to as a "portal." A door's essential and primary purpose is to provide security by controlling the portal (doorway). Once the door is open or left unsecured, a predator can come in freely to take, rearrange, and destroy your possessions. The predator I'm speaking of is the enemy of your soul (the devil), and his goal is to bind, break down, and build an altar to himself with your life. He does this by detaining you spiritually as a hostage, destroying your identity, and devouring your purpose by utilizing your flesh and the words of others against you.

Matthew 12:29 (NKJV): 29 Or how can one enter a strong man's house and plunder his goods, unless he first binds the strong man? And then he will plunder his house.

The process continued until I took a turn onto the journey of healing. Healing begins with accepting that you're in bondage. Healing can begin once you realize you are wounded and seek intervention for the wound. I am a nurse practitioner by occupation. God has given me spiritual wisdom and medical knowledge and the ability to relate that knowledge to the spiritual realm. In order to provide the proper treatment for an injury, the first thing we do as clinicians in the medical field is to assess the situation. This is done by obtaining objective and subjective data. Objective data are what you can measure or visualize, and subjective data are the description of the symptoms or feelings. Once I began analyzing my symptoms, emotions, and behaviors, I discovered that the root cause of my heart wound was unforgiveness.

Initially the door to unforgiveness was opened when my parents divorced; I held this unforgiveness in my heart against both my father and my mother. This cycle continued because as a result of this unforgiveness, I utilized crippling self-talk. "You don't understand."

"You have not been through what I went through." "You don't know what they did to me." "I can't just let it go." "It's their problem, not mine." I was also critical and negative toward others. I would find fault in others to justify my internal pain. I adopted both of these unhealthy coping mechanisms because I did not want to face reality but mask how I really was feeling. I wanted others to endure the pain I was feeling; this made me feel as if I was gaining something although in reality I was losing everything and everyone around me. My wounds were not healing but growing more infected because I was unaware of the internalized hurt and pain.

Unforgiveness is manifested once emotional trauma (e.g., divorce, rape, etc.) has occurred. If the trauma was never healed by God, the seed it sprouts is then watered with hurt, pain, grief, and complexity. Next the seed is nurtured/fertilized with depression, anxiety, mistrust, and confusion, thereby giving birth to unforgiveness. If unforgiveness is unresolved, the root of bitterness springs forth. Bitterness is a deeply rooted anger enhanced by grudge as a result of emotional trauma (a fortified wall within the heart).

Hebrews 12:14–15 (NKJV): 14 Pursue peace with all people, and holiness, without which no one will see the Lord: 15 looking carefully lest anyone fall short of the grace of God; lest any root of bitterness springing up cause trouble, and by this many become defiled.

If the root of bitterness is not healed, the individual will build a wall of resistance in the heart. This resistance becomes fortified (strengthened to prevent attacks). The fortification of the heart is a defense mechanism to prevent the person/s from being hurt again by way of deception. A wall is placed at the heart gate whereby love cannot be received or reciprocated. The love you experience or have with your children, spouse, and others is contaminated (impure). Genuine love cannot be demonstrated because the heart is defiled, which contaminates the thoughts, intentions, and behaviors of the individual's identity and/or personality.

Matthew 5:14–16 (NKJV): 14 "You are the light of the world. A city that is set on a hill cannot be hidden. 15 Nor do they light a lamp and put it under a basket, but on a lamp stand, and it gives light to all who are in the house. 16 Let your light so shine before men, that they may see your good works and glorify your Father in heaven.

The Scriptures tell us we are to be the light of the world, but when the root of bitterness is in operation, it obscures or dims our light of joy and leaves our soul in a darkened state. God lovingly desires that we pursue peace and live holy lives. We pursue peace by receiving healing from our past traumatic experiences and internalized hurts. It is God's desire that we as human beings become whole in our body, soul, and spirit. When we are whole, we can demonstrate His image and likeness on the earth.

An Analogy of the Hidden Root Properties

Germination is the process by which a plant grows from a seed. While germination is taking place, you cannot see this process because it takes place under the earth or soil once a seed has been planted.

1. When the seed of emotional trauma is sown, the seed begins to germinate.

2. The seed is watered by adversity, guilt, shame, condemnation, etc.

3. These adversities apply pressure to the seed and cracks begin to appear.

4. The soul becomes fragmented, allowing the root to grow.

5. If not healed, delivered, and set free from this yoke of bondage, the root continues to grow until the bitterness springs forth.

6. Your heart is the soil, the seed is unforgiveness, and the root is bitterness, which takes deep root within the heart. This root continues to grow until it chokes the life (abundant life) out of you.

Steps in Process of Germination

♦ Water is absorbed by seed

♦ The seed coat is cracked by water, growth is activated

♦ Root begins to grow downward into soil (hypocotyl)

♦ Stem shoot begins to grow upward towards the sun (epicotyl)

♦ Growth continues, shoot grows green leaves (photmorphogenesis)

Internal stressors that open the door to unforgiveness are abuse (sexual, physical, mental, or verbal), rape, divorce, adultery, death, and offense. The enemy will utilize these internal stressors as distractions. His goal is to keep your mind fixated on what has happened in your past so that you become stagnant and comfortable with regression instead of progressing. Once we allow him to do so, we are unable to pursue our divine appointed destiny. If I had not endured the darkness, I would not have appreciated the light!

We must know that we are temples purchased with the precious blood of Jesus Christ. But we must also know that Satan is privy to this information as well, therefore he seeks to desecrate the temple (our bodies) with acts of sin, iniquity, and transgression. Satan is a spirit and spirits must have a body to carry out their deceptive, diabolical plots. This is why he has to have a body to implement his perverted plan. The body he utilizes is a person who oftentimes is someone you are familiar with. Satan will utilize an agent from within to cause your downfall. He will utilize a person who knows you well enough to befriend, behold, and berate you by purporting to trust and respect you.

1 Corinthians 2:16 (NKJV): Do you not know that you are the temple of God and that the Spirit of God dwells in you?

This scripture ends with a question mark. Oftentimes we do not know who we are, who we belong to, and who resides inside of us. Our invisible enemy, Satan, desires to keep this a secret so that he can emotionally manipulate us with the desires of our flesh. A secret will keep you bound to shackles and Satan. The flesh is weak and wars against the spirit, which is the Holy Spirit that dwells within us. The flesh seeks to gratify our desires, and the spirit seeks to glorify God the Father. These desires are usually unhealthy, ungodly, and unrighteous. Desires are distractions attached to a detonator that can, if allowed, destroy, debilitate, and distract you from reaching your God-ordained dreams, ambitions, and plans.

Perception

Perception is what the physical eye can only see.

Distorted information has found its way into my brain,

Many unspeakable thoughts I dare not to explain.

Sadness enslaved my mind and pain captivated my heart.

I can't seem to break free, oh how, when, and where do I start?

Sin has ensnared me, held tightly under its locking key.

Let me go, I plea. I must break free to become who He has called me

to be.

CHAPTER 5

Distractions

Our lives are filled with so many distractions, and being in the world does not make it any easier. These distractions seek to appease our flesh.

1 John 2: 15–17 (KJV): 15 Do not love the world or the things in the world. If anyone loves the world, the love of the Father is not in him. 16 For all that is in the world—the lust of the flesh, the lust of the eyes, and the pride of life—is not of the Father but is of the world. 17 And the world is passing away, and the lust of it, but he who does the will of God abides forever.

These three temptations—lust of the flesh, lust of the eyes, and the pride of life—are attached to the world. If we allow them to seduce and ensnare us, they will place us on the path called destruction, and the final destination is a dead end (death). We must be aware that all humans will face these three areas of temptations; they will be presented before the act of sin is committed. Before we are tempted, the enemy will package it in an unusually elaborate package with a big red bow and present it to us. Usually the things he places before us are what our fleshly nature desires. To break this down further, here are three examples of temptations.

A) Lust of the flesh: Sexual sins, gossip, physical violence, and drug use.

B) Lust of the eyes: Watching pornography, coveting other's belongings, wanting another's wife or husband as King David did with Bathsheba (2 Samuel 11:2).

C) Pride of life: Being prideful, boastful, or arrogant, desiring credit for another's work, desiring to be esteemed by people and above others, wanting to be worshipped or validated (e.g., Satan desiring to be worshipped).

Pride was an issue with Lucifer (Satan) while he still lived in Heaven. His pride got the best of him, and he decided to rebel against God. As a result, he was banished from Heaven. After his dismissal from Heaven, he was hurled onto the earth, where he now reigns and seeks to deceive mankind through distractions and sin, which gratify the desires of man. In other words, his goal is to utilize the love you have for people and objects against you in order to kill, steal, and destroy by any means necessary, as I mentioned earlier!

Isaiah 14:13–14 (NKJV) 13 For you have said in your heart: "I will ascend into heaven, I will exalt my throne above the stars of God; I will also sit on the mount of the congregation the farthest sides of the north; 14 I will ascend above the heights of the clouds, I will be like the Most High."

We must realize that if we allow it, sin will lead us down a path of temporary happiness, depression, oppression, regression, frustrations, hurts, unforgiveness, sadness, emotional distress, bitterness, rejection, shame, and pain that will result in spiritual and physical death if we don't allow the light of the Father to illuminate the detoured dark paths. These are the different situations I've encountered when I've decided to choose my own path.

Distractions were a major change of course in my life. I was distracted with what the world has to offer: sex, perversion, money, lust, and all types of temptations. When I think of the world today as it is, it's a cesspool with a deceptive sign posted next to it: "Enter without risk." And this is what I did. I entered without knowing the risk. My journey continued as a long, winding road full of twist and turns. During this ride I allowed Satan to utilize my emotions, desires, and passions to magnify these distractions, indulging in them willingly and ignorantly.

At the age of eighteen I decided to move out and obtain my first apartment. Eighteen for many is a milestone on the way to adulthood; at this age I began to feel arrogant, invincible, and intelligent. I thought I knew a whole lot and quickly found out I knew a whole lot of nothing! In other words, what I perceived as reality was actually deceit and manipulation. I began consuming alcohol and smoking marijuana. If you've had any experience with these two drugs, you know they increase your appetite for sex and perversion. Therefore, the quest for love continued, disguised by sex; I equated good sex with love. As an illustration, it was during this time that the alcohol and weed had a conversation with my pulsating vagina and my vagina with my delusional, debased mind. I had no control over my flesh, for it had me as its slave, and I yielded to its every request, which had me on a path to destruction.

John 8:34 (NKJV) 34 Jesus answered them, "Most assuredly, I say to you, whoever commits sin is a slave of sin."

Notice I stated that I allowed Satan to utilize my desires, emotions, and passions against me. I say this because Satan does not make us do anything against our will. He simply tempts us with a particular thing or person, and it's up to us whether we take the bait. Temptation simply put is the presentation of evil. Satan's goal is to present gifts to us, appearing delightful. But the truth of the matter is that the actual purpose of the gift is masked or concealed. Underneath the mask the gift is perverted and its purpose is to gratify your fleshly nature or desires. He does this illegally in the aspiration of luring us out of our Father's will and house into sin, and once in sin we become a slave to it (bondage). As I mentioned earlier, Satan will present a package that is decorated and elaborately sealed with a big red bow and once we open the package, we are in for a rude awakening! Inside the box are alluring, tantalizing trinkets that will produce and replicate sin. Inside the box of trinkets are abandonment, accusations, anger, bitterness, broken dreams, chaos, confusion, depression, despair, detriment, empty promises, hate, hurt, manipulation, mistrust, trauma, shame, rejection, and resentment, to name a few. We must come to the realization that if Satan was bold enough to approach our Father (Jesus) and tempt Him, in like manner he will utilize the same scheme with us. In other words, he has **no** new tricks or trinkets!

Often, when we are enslaved to sin, we have no knowledge of this, and this is right where the enemy would have us to be, ignorant to his devices. I was that slave, and ignorantly I indulged in what the world has to offer. As a matter of fact, it was as if I was a puppet and Satan was the puppeteer pulling the strings that pleased my flesh. Yielding to my flesh hid my true identity, the called and chosen Erica was tucked away, and therefore I was unable to access the will God had for my life. My thoughts, intentions, will, and emotions were controlled by my sinful nature. In addition, the past hurts and pain were so deep and real, I needed a temporary way of escape. My escape routes were alcohol, drugs, lust, pleasure, and sex. While traveling down the different escape routes, I came to discover that I was suffering from the need to be loved. The need to be loved caused me to search for love in the most unusual places. Under the circumstances, feeling rejected and unloved, and rehearsing the mental, physical, and sexual abuse I had endured within my mind, I was on a tumultuous quest. With this in mind, I detoured onto the roads of teenage pregnancy, low self-esteem, depression, and suicidal thoughts in hopes of ending the immeasurable, intense pain I was feeling.

Reflecting on the times I felt I was in love with a man, I now know it was an illusion because I was bruised, broken, and unable to receive or reciprocate love. I could not give that which was a deficit within my life. I equated love with how good the sex was, thereby falling in love with every man who could give me prolific, pleasurable sexual ecstasy. Many broken women equate love to how a man makes them feel between the sheets. Ladies, this is not love but lust! Women, we must break this cycle of emotional manipulation, meaning our emotions are manipulated by the multiple orgasms we experience while having sex with a man who is not in love with us. Some men will become whoever they need to become to bribe you out of your prized possession, your valuable vagina. Once we have given a man our vagina, what else priceless do you have to offer? We must stop selling ourselves as cheap and invaluable. After we have given a man our vagina and he no longer desires to be with us, rejection joins in and takes a ride on the back of sex. After the sexual thrill is gone, it leaves behind its friend rejection.

Rejection will manifest in different forms. For me it was seeking to be loved, to end the deep-rooted pain that consumed my life. In a quest for love and to cover the pain, I desired to have a child; I thought this child would give me the love I so desperately wanted and needed. With this in mind, I became pregnant two weeks before my nineteenth birthday. The pregnancy was a result of indulging in a week of weed and unprotected sex that turned into a long-distance relationship. Initially I did not know I was pregnant, but I displayed some symptoms. I was sleeping frequently throughout the day and I was feeling very fatigued. The father of my child told me I was pregnant because I was having morning sickness, a term I did not fully understand at the time.

Being pregnant with my first child was delightful. I was so excited about being a mother and having someone to love and love me back, I did not take into consideration the resilience it would take to raise a child as a single parent. Life as a single parent was not easy. I was left to figure out how I would provide physically, mentally, and financially for this little person who was innocent and precious. I knew I wanted to give my child a loving and caring home, but this did not come easily because I found myself working and going to school to pursue a career as a nurse. My baby was in the background of my life. During his young years I sought to give him the best life possible at his expense. Even in the midst of my seeking my desires, God had a perfect plan for our lives.

I became a single parent because I was looking to fill a void that at the time I did not realize was a void. I was desperately seeking to be loved, not realizing that I had yet to learn how to love myself. As humans we desire to feel the intangible presence of love; however, if our hearts are infiltrated with past hurts, we are unable to express love in its purest form. At the age of twenty-four, I decided to move to Jacksonville, Florida, to be with my son's father. My desire was for us to get married and live happily ever after—at least that was the plan. Plan A came to fruition, but the second part of plan A did not. After we married, I quickly realized we were not good for one another. Instead of living in a home furnished with love and happiness, I was living in House of Hell Marriage. Because all we did was argue and fight, the home was infused with chaos, confusion, distrust, and infidelity.

Love is a word that produces an expressive action. If you don't receive love, you're unable to reciprocate love. Not understanding the true essence of love caused me to stay in a marriage not built on love. Being scarred from the divorce of my parents, I chose to endure the physical, verbal, and mental abuse because I did not want my children to endure the pain I felt at the age of eleven when my parents divorced. The pain they were being exposed to, though, was much more damaging. Many days I would go to work with not one black eye but two because I needed the money to pay bills and feed my children, and at this time I was pregnant with my third child. Often my coworkers would whisper behind my back about the facial bruising. The manager of the deli/bakery where I worked as a cake decorator would try to convince me to go home, but I would refuse because I desperately needed money to provide shelter, food, and clothing for my children. As a result, I chose to disregard the whispers and gossip right under my nose.

It was a cold December day in Florida and I had to catch two different buses to get to work. My daily routine was to put both of my sons in a stroller made for one child and walk to the bus stop. I was three months pregnant with my daughter, and on this particular day I had decided to end my life, my two sons' and unborn child lives. My suicidal plan was to throw my two sons in the St. John's River and jump behind them. During this time in my life, I was so broken I felt I had nothing more to live for, and although I had my children, my mind at the time could not comprehend that they were my blessing and my strength. Major depression had obscured my thought process so that I contemplated taking my children's lives and mine as well. My invisible driver, Satan, had turned onto Suicidal Court, which ran into Death Cul-de-sac. Depression can cause you to become so disconnected from reality that you no longer desire to deal with the atmosphere around you in a healthy state. Depression had me delusional and my soul was fragmented (shattered).

When a soul is fragmented, a shattering of the heart has taken place, causing the true identity that God created and purposed for that individual to become lost. Once the identity is lost, the person becomes a different person (physically, mentally, and spiritually). The triune man's homeostatic state is disrupted (body, soul, and spirit). *Homeostasis* is defined as the tendency toward a relatively stable equilibrium between interdependent elements, especially as maintained by physiological processes. It's the ability to maintain a stable environment, and during this time of my life I was unable to maintain a stable environment. I felt as if death was the only escape route from all the hellacious misery and pain. I was at the edge of the cliff ready to jump; all I could think of was that I wanted the pain and misery to end. Obliviously I did not go through with my plan.

God had another route for me to take instead, a route that was a rough ride, but it catapulted me into His purpose. If you are reading this book and contemplating suicide, please seek help immediately. Suicide is a permanent solution to a temporary problem! Ladies, realize you are a priceless jewel, so priceless Jesus gave His life so that you and I can live an abundant life! I call you to rise now in Jesus's name and SOAR above every storm, opposition, accusation, rejection, pain, and past traumatic event that attempts to STOP your divine alignment with your destiny. I say, arise, my sister!

Special Note: If you are experiencing suicidal ideations, please call immediately the National Suicide Prevention Lifeline: 1-800-273-8255 or 911.

Unknown Love

Looking for love in the most unusual places,

I can't find what I have never felt

Or give what was not dealt.

Knowing not what to expect,

More is less and less is more.

Just don't know, must I continue to explore?

CHAPTER 6

God's Purpose

Are you wondering what kept me from committing suicide? It was an angel of the Lord! After arriving downtown to the bus station, I got off of the first bus and was waiting on the next bus to arrive. A lady that appeared to be homeless sat down beside me and began speaking to me. She was very descriptive while explaining to me about my past, present, and future. At the time my body was there, but my mind was disassociated. I was existing and not living. Nothing she said raised my interest or awareness. But what intrigued me was when the bus came to take me to my final destination, the bag lady assisted me onto the bus, and before she got off the bus, she said, "Erica, remember God loves you." She said goodbye and called each one of my son's by name. She also told me I was pregnant with a female child. This mysterious person also knew I desired to commit suicide, she explained that God called me to live and not die. In other words, my life has purpose although I was paralyzed by pain. She stepped down off of the bus and waved at us and suddenly she vanished.

At the time I was unaware she was an angel. The first person I saw was my children's daycare provider, so I told her about this unusual lady. Her response was, "that was an angel." The next person I shared this strange experience with was my manager, and of course she repeated those exact words. This encounter was a heavenly visitation, for the night before I had fervently cried out to God to show me He is real because I wanted to believe there is a God. I desired proof of His existence. After leaving work, I had hopes of seeing this lady once more, but I never saw her again.

My decision to move to Jacksonville was motivated by unorganized emotions for I had not prayed prior to making this decision, neither did I receive my parents' blessing. When I shared with them my desire to move, they were totally against it. What may seem to some as stepping out on faith was actually stepping out on failure.

Once I decided to leave the ark of safety, I was exposed to the elements of the world, enticed and tempted by the enemy, which led me down one path that had two forks in the road that led to destruction and death. The cul-de-sac I ended up on that appeared to be death was actually a way of escape. I was able to do a three-point turn back to the Father, Son, and Holy Spirit. Once I turned around I began to see a glimpse of light that I recognized as my Father. The passenger (Satan) who became the driver had obstructed my view along with my fleshly desires, therefore he hindered me from seeing my Father in the rearview mirror. I could not see, hear, smell, or taste the Son, or reach my hand in the direction of the Holy Spirit so He could lead and guide me back to truth and safety. I was unaware of the impending danger—my senses and perception were distorted.

My other four senses were also unable to detect the danger. The sense of thermoception that detects heat and cold did not detect the invisible passenger was hot and had on gasoline underwear, which ignited my dormant passions. The sense of equilibrioception was distorted for I could not comprehend that my life was unbalanced and that I had taken the wrong route on my journey. The sense of nociception was not able to sense the pain I caused my Heavenly Father, my earthly parents, my children, and myself. Last but not least, my sense of proprioception was unable to realize that my hands were above my head in a posture of surrender, and yet I would not allow the Holy Spirit to lead me back to the correct path, the path of righteousness.

Proverbs 4:26–27 (NKJV): 26 Ponder the path of your feet and let all your ways be established. 27 Do not turn to the right or the left. Remove your foot from evil.

Although I was not equipped for the journey, my Father knew the course I would take, for that long trip catapulted me into my purpose. He chose me before the foundation of the world to be where I am today!!!

Romans 8:30 (NKJV): 30 Moreover whom He predestined, these He also called; whom He called, these He also justified; and whom He justified, these He also glorified.

As children of the Most High God, we must come to the knowledge and understanding that we can only rely on and receive reality through the eyesight of God the Father, the Son, and the Holy Spirit. An analogy for this is placing someone else's glasses upon your face so that you can see, only to realize that everything in front of you is blurry. You may cleanse the lens, but your attempt is unsuccessful and your vision remains fuzzy because you have on someone else's glasses and you are attempting to see your purpose through another's vision! This was my story. I was living my life based on what others wanted and thought of me. I was attempting to start this journey called life without circumspect, taking risks, at the request of others, and of my flesh, not fully understanding that I was ignoring God's plans for my life. God has a plan and a purpose for each of our lives; however, if we are wearing the wrong glasses, we will become blinded by what's in front of us.

Jeremiah 29:11 (NKJV) 11 For I know the thoughts that I think toward you, says the Lord, thoughts of peace and not of evil, to give you a future and a hope.

It is our Heavenly Father's plan to get us off on the right start, but along the way sin creeps in and changes our course of direction and our destination. During the journey we may have starts, stops, procrastinations, layovers, sleepovers, and do-overs. We may find ourselves going around, and round, up, and down that same mountain because we will not allow the finished work of the cross to resonate within our hearts and minds. We would rather unsuccessfully fight the Goliaths in our lives with our personal strengths and capabilities, instead of relying on the strength of God. Ultimately, I was attempting to do everything as it relates to my life in my human will and not allowing the will of the Father to take precedence. I never knew "I could do all things through Christ which strengthens me" (Philippians 4:13). Only through opposition and adversity could I really understand that I could do nothing in my strength and that it is only when we are weak that His strength is made perfect within us.

When I think of strength, I picture a strong tower that is impenetrable and cannot be destroyed. This is who God is. He is the powerful, impenetrable, and unstoppable force that keeps us on the narrow path to life eternal, if we will surrender and grab hold of His hand. Only when I decided to dwell in the secret place of His tabernacle did I become fortified in Him. Once I decided to take off the wrong glasses and accept Jesus's perception as the only reality, He allowed me to see beyond seeing; my vision and purpose became crystal clear. The mysteries of my life began unfolding and the furniture within my spiritual house began rearranging and transitioning. I immediately terminated the enemy's driving privileges indefinitely and gave him an immediate eviction notice to vacate the premises of my life and my spiritual house. In fact, once this was done, I went to the Father through the Son's name, repented of my sins, and asked the Father for forgiveness. The Father granted me immunity from my self-inflicted death sentence.

1 John 1:9 New International Version (NIV): 9 If we confess our sins, he is faithful and just and will forgive us our sins and purify us from all unrighteousness.

Once I made the choice to surrender my will to the will of the Father and accept and embrace the purpose He had predestined for me, I began to SOAR in Him. **S**tanding on His Word, **O**perating in His Truth, **A**ctivating His Word, and **R**eleasing His Word over my life, I began to mount on wings as an eagle. Undoubtedly God the Father became my new driver and God the Son was my dwelling place. God the Holy Spirit was my GPS (global positioning system). The Holy Spirit would now become the guide who would lead me into all spirit and truth. He assured me that during tough times He would be my comforter, my teacher, my intercessor, and the one who will bring all things back to my remembrance (He will not allow me to forget the price the Son paid in exchange for my life). And if I just so happen to get lost, the Son would lead me back on the narrow path of eternal life. Suddenly, restoration, regeneration, reformation, and realignment began taking place deep within my heart, deep within my inner man.

John 14:6 (NIV): Jesus answered, "I am the way and the truth and the life. No one comes to the Father except through me."

Not Forsaken

Behold I stand at the door and knock.

Please let me in so I can stop the clock.

For Father Time waits for no one; you've wasted enough time

Because the Prince of the Air has kept you blind and manipulated
your mind.

Trials and tribulations you've encountered because you went left when
I instructed you to go right.

If you seek my face daily, it is here that you would enter into my light.

You have been looking for love in all the wrong places and I have been
here all the time, for I told you I would never leave nor forsake you!

You see my child, everything that you need lies within Me, for it was
done at Calvary.

CHAPTER 7

-

Home Is Where Jesus Lives

I hope by now you have come to discover there's a new driver who brought along two other passengers to make the trip unforgettable, peaceful, and life changing. This new driver took me from a low state and catapulted me to a place of SOARING! In the car with me was God the Father (Pilot), God the Son (Copilot), and God the Holy Spirit (Autopilot). I have surrendered and granted God full access to create in me a clean heart and to renew a steadfast spirit, just as King David desired in Psalm 51:10. My accepting Jesus as my Savior allowed me to become a new creature and discover that my identity and existence are found in Him!

Acts 17:28 (NKJV): 28 For in Him we live and move and have our being, as also some of your own poets have said, "For we are also His offspring."

John 14:26 (NIV): 26 But the Advocate, the Holy Spirit, whom the Father will send in my name, will teach you all things and will remind you of everything I have said to you.

This trip was harmonious, as we all worked together to promote and pursue the purpose the Father has for me. During this trip my journey was pleasant and very exciting, and the sightseeing along the way was amazing, to say the least. While on this journey God began to resuscitate, rebuild, and restructure my spiritual foundation. Jesus began to intervene, illuminate, and implement a plan for not only my physical life but for my eternal life as well! The Holy Spirit began to reveal, teach, and intercede for me. The Holy Spirit is our GPS; He always knows the shortest and most efficient route. For the first time I was able to hear the Father's voice clearly. My ear gates were uninterrupted by the luring words of the devil. The utterance and breath of His vivacious words breathed life and fulfillment back into my once limp and lifeless body. As He spoke to me, the very essence of His words became life in the midst of what I perceived as a dead and hopeless mess. God used my mess to write a new story, my life, my story, for His Glory! The missing pieces of the pages of my life were mended and rewritten. The crumbled and torn pages began to reappear with a colorful format, distinct handwriting, a new message, and a peculiar title.

2 Corinthians 5:17 (KJV):17 Therefore if any man be in Christ, he is a new creature: old things are passed away; behold all things are become new.

When things are new, they are exciting, fun, and delightful. Once I allowed God to establish new beginnings in my life, I was no longer satisfied with life as I once knew it. I sought out opportunities to share this newfound life with others; I wanted everyone around me to experience this joy and precious treasure I had stumbled upon. When we allow God to take the wheel in our lives, we will notice that the ride is much smoother and that He has already made provision for your destination. During the ride He is constantly reminding us that He's preparing a place for us within His Father's kingdom and that we too will occupy this place.

John 14 (NIV) 1–4: Do not let your hearts be troubled. You believe in God; believe also in me. 2 My Father's house has many rooms; if that were not so, would I have told you that I am going there to prepare a place for you? 3 And if I go and prepare a place for you, I will come back and take you to be with me that you also may be where I am. 4 You know the way to the place where I am going.

The only way we can be assured that we know the way to the place where Jesus resides is to keep our hearts, minds, thoughts, eyes, and ears inclined to His word. We must also stay hidden and seated deep within Him. When we are hidden in Christ, Jesus fights our battles. Jesus wants us to know Him in His fullness; He wants us to be familiar with His voice thereby not being led astray or taken captive by the enemy's diabolic ploys. We must not fall victim to his lies, deceit, schemes, and manipulation. We must recognize and discern the voice and the heart of Jesus!

The Scriptures declare in John 10:27–28 (KJV): 27 My sheep hear my voice, and I know them, and they follow me: 28 And I give unto them eternal life; and they shall never perish, neither shall any man pluck them out of my hand.

I am not a builder in the physical sense of building a home, but I know building a house does not come easy or free. It comes with a price. Once a person decides to build a house, they must go through an approval process that can be time-consuming and costly. During the process sacrifices and commitments must be made and met. In addition, the builder himself must ensure the land on which the house is to be built is stable and firm before pouring the foundation. Once we surrender and accept salvation through Jesus Christ, we have secured our heavenly home. Our foundation is secure and no longer unstable.

Jesus paid the price for all mankind with His precious blood on the cross. Our lives are likened to building a house. Before the building can be erected, our foundation must be secure and stable. To complete the building process, we must surrender our will to that of the Father, accept the Son as our personal Lord and Savior (salvation), and sacrifice our life, thoughts, desires, emotions, agendas, etc. to the functioning of the Holy Spirit. It's a must that we are willing to completely submit everything to Jesus.

Ephesians 2:19–22 (NIV): 19 Consequently, you are no longer foreigners and strangers, but fellow citizens with God's people and also members of his household, 20 built on the foundation of the apostles and prophets, with Christ Jesus himself as the chief cornerstone. 21 In him the whole building is joined together and rises to become a holy temple in the Lord. 22 And in him you too are being built together to become a dwelling in which God lives by his Spirit.

While building your spiritual house upon His foundation, He delightfully demonstrates His love, explains the next step, and ensures that you understand and that you're familiar with His voice. He desires that we all come to the knowledge that He is the only way, that His word is truth, and that He is the light that dissipates all darkness. You see, when I left my Father's house, the way back grew dim. I forgot His word was the only truth, and as a result, my life/spiritual house was filled with darkness. This darkness consisted of sin, broken dreams, and empty promises. This repetitive, whirlwind journey was filled with unwanted twists, turns, detours, and what I thought was my final destination. It was only when I dead ended onto Death Cul-de-sac that I discovered it was only through the end of me that He could be! I discovered I am a child of the Most High God and not what man perceives or wants me to be. The Holy Spirit revealed that we must love who He is in order to love who we are. Only through my emptiness could He fill every voided place within me with His comforting Spirit.

Once I decided to accept I was broken, weak, wounded, and a sinner, He was able to destroy the works of the devil that I had allowed to take me captive. I thank God for loving me with an intense *agape* love, for sending Jesus to rescue me out of entrapment orchestrated by the enemy. I am grateful for the Holy Spirit grabbing hold of my hand and leading me back home where I belong, safe and secure in my Father's house. The building of my spiritual house was not easy, and it cost me a lot of pain along the way. Indeed, the one who paid the most—and no, it was not free—is my Father Jesus Christ, who shed His blood in exchange for you and me in a place called Calvary!

There are two paths in life you can take, one which leads to your purpose and the dark winding diverted path that leads to pain. Although we can do things to get our lives off the course in which God intended, God still has a perfect plan and purpose for each of our lives. My destiny destination began with turbulence but I discovered along my journey that the price Jesus paid was far greater than the pain I had endured locating my purpose. I now know that God has planned, prepared, and purposed all of our lives before the foundations of the world. God will never give up on us, we give up on ourselves by not trusting or seeking Him for His direction to be established in our lives. His desire is to get us to an expected place, a place created and designated for you and I. We must know that God is concerned with every intricate detail of our lives and desires that we become knowledgably of His desires and learn very valuable lessons found in His Holy word.

Valuable Lessons I Learned

1. **First Lesson: I will never leave you nor forsake you.**

Hebrews 13:5 New King James Version (NKJV) *Let your* conduct *be* without covetousness; *be* content with such things as you have. For He Himself has said, "I will never leave you nor forsake you." (I coveted the world desires and felt as if I was missing out, I was not content with the way of life that my Father provided, therefore I left my father's house likened unto the prodigal son).

2. **Second Lesson: I have overcome the world.**

John 16:33 New King James Version (NKJV)33. These things I have spoken to you, that in Me you may have peace. In the world, you will have tribulation; but be of good cheer, I have overcome the world." (I had become so comfortable being a part of the world and indulging in its desires until I could not discern that all the hell and tribulations that I'd encountered, He overcame and defeated them all with His precious blood).

3. **Third Lesson: Blessed is the man who endures temptation (presentation of evil).**

James 1:12-15 New King James Version (NKJV)12 Blessed *is* the man who endures temptation; for when he has been approved, he will receive the crown of life which the Lord has promised to those who love Him. 13 Let no one say when he is tempted, "I am tempted by God"; for God cannot be tempted by evil, nor does He Himself tempt anyone. 14 But each one is tempted when he is drawn away by his own desires and enticed. 15 Then, when desire has conceived, it gives birth to sin; and sin, when it is full-grown, brings forth death. (I allowed Satan to utilize and manipulate my desires, emotions, and passions against me, which in return caused my self-destruction).

Now that we have reached our final destination, I truly hope you have enjoyed this adventurous journey into my life. I pray that you have discovered that your destiny is found in the creator (God). The time has come for us to depart from one another; however, if you have not identified your destiny, it's a must that you continue your quest and find your treasure chest!

Proverbs 24:3–4 (NKJV): 3 Through wisdom a house is built, and by understanding it is established;4 by knowledge the rooms are filled with all precious and pleasant riches.

Hebrews 3:1–6 (NIV): Therefore, holy brothers and sisters who share in the heavenly calling fix your thoughts on Jesus, whom we acknowledge as our apostle and high priest. 2 He was faithful to the one who appointed him, just as Moses was faithful in all God's house. 3 Jesus has been found worthy of greater honor than Moses, just as the builder of a house has greater honor than the house itself. 4 For every house is built by someone, but God is the builder of everything. 5 Moses was faithful as a servant in all God's house, bearing witness to what would be spoken by God in the future. 6 But Christ is faithful as the Son over God's house. And we are his house, if indeed we hold firmly to our confidence and the hope in which we glory.

Chosen

I chose you, why can't you see?

It began long before I formed and framed the world.

My plan consisted of you hidden in Me.

Before I knitted you in your mother's womb, I chose you to be a girl

Who would accomplish My plan to heal the land.

You strayed away—that was not My plan.

You became entangled, ensnared, and trapped in a foreign land

Because you yielded to the voice of a stranger

Embedded with death, destruction, and danger.

Despite Me shedding My blood on Calvary; it was all I had left

To pour out for you as a sacrifice.

It was the ultimate price to save your life!

LETTER TO THE READER

My beautiful, fearfully, and wonderfully made sister, I honor and salute you for not giving up and for continuing to run this race with strength, resiliency, and perseverance. When God created you He knew the exact plans He had for you. No, you are not a mistake, for He created you to speak life into others as yourself. He knew before the earth was established you would be the apple of His eye and that your family, friends, and community need your vital presence. As women we nurture and pour ourselves out to others. Even when our cisterns are diminished, we continue to pour and share our living waters with those who are undeserving and those who are not our husbands. As a result, we are left feeling empty, voided, and unworthy. We begin to lose faith, sight, and hope. It is water that gives life, and when our cisterns are shallow and/or depleted, we are unable to focus on the purpose and vision He has imputed to us.

The vision and purpose that was inside of you at birth remains, my sister, you must remember that the Spirit of God is upon the face of the waters (you), and He desires to bring light into those voided and dark areas. We can never find light and life in futile desires. Illumination is limited when we seek our vision by way of a man: our children, our husbands, our friends, and others for the source of light exist only in God. Ultimately, sister, God desires that you no longer thirst naturally or spiritually, for He has birthed inside of you rivers of living water and desires to fill you continually if you're willing to align your will to His will and stay in His presence, for He is the fountain of everlasting Life!

PRAYER

Father, I ask that you forgive me for depleting my cistern and giving out to those who were undeserving. I ask, Father, that you grant me the ability to hear your voice, obey your instructions, and follow the blueprint you have designed for my life. Father, I ask that you replenish and fill the void and empty areas in my life. Father, I ask that you recapture the broken pieces of me that I left with those who abandoned, abused, belittled, controlled, deceived, hurt, manipulated, and rejected me. Father, I thank you for restoring my body, soul, and spirit back to their original intended state. Father, teach me how to love others and you with all my heart, soul, mind, and strength. Father, I ask you also to teach me how to put my trust, faith, and hope only in you and not man. Father, I thank you for replenishing my cistern and restoring my sight to carry out the vision and purpose you have for my life. I decree and declare I am filled with your rivers of living water that shall flow from me continually in Jesus name. Amen!

SALVATION PRAYER

After reading this book, if you know within your heart that you have not submitted your life to Jesus Christ as your Lord and Savior and/or you have backslid, please repeat this prayer of salvation. Father in Heaven, I come before your throne in Jesus's name acknowledging that I am a sinner in need of a Savior. I repent of my sins and the life I have lived outside of you. I ask, Father, that you forgive me of my sins, iniquities, and transgressions. I ask, Father, that you give me the desire to live a life that's pleasing unto you, a life of righteousness and holiness, set aside to do your will. I believe Jesus Christ is your only begotten Son, He shed His blood on the cross for remission of my sin, he was dead for three days in the belly of the earth, but on the third day He rose so that I would have the right to the Tree of Life. Father, your word in Romans 10:9 states, "If I confess Lord Jesus and believe with my heart that God raised Jesus from the dead, I shall be saved." Father, I now confess with my mouth that Jesus is Lord and that God raised Him from the dead. I accept Him as my personal Savior from this day forth. I ask that you come into my heart and live. I thank you that my life is transformed and that I am a new creature in Christ. Heavenly Father, I thank you for granting me eternal life in Jesus name. Amen!

Scriptural References: Genesis 1:1–5, John 4:1–26, John 7:38, and Mark 12:30

ABOUT THE AUTHOR

Erica Williams was born in Phenix City, Alabama. She's the wife of a retired army veteran who served our country for twenty years, the mother of four beautiful children—three sons and one daughter and the grandmother of eight grandchildren.

She is the founder of Resilient Rose Holistic Ministry and founder/pastor of United in Christ International Ministries (UICIM).

Her ministry extends to healing as she is a nurse practitioner (MSN) and has been serving in the medical field for twenty-six years. Currently she's pursuing her doctoral degree at Troy University.

Erica was ordained and licensed by Frontline Theological Seminary, earning a bachelor of arts degree in pastoral ministry.

Erica has a passionate desire for God's people to be healed, delivered, and set free from demonic yokes and strongholds. She believes that through prayer, deliverance, inner healing, supplication, and fasting, God's people can and will be set free from the manipulation of the enemy.

Erica provides outreach in the community, assisting with donating school supplies, feeding the homeless, praying for the sick, donating to the poor, and comforting those who have had catastrophic losses in their lives. She believes the church is not confined to a building because God's people are the church.

Erica's faith and trust in God are the foundational principles by which she lives. She knows that according to Philippians 4:13 (KJV), she can do all things through Christ who strengthened her.

NOTES

1. McLeod, S. A. (2018, May 03). Erik erikson's stages of psychosocial development. Simply Psychology. https://www.simplypsychology.org/Erik-Erikson.html

2. " rape." Merriam-Webster.com. 2020. https://www.merriam-webster.com (1May 2020).

3. " stockholm syndrome." Merriam-Webster.com. 2020. https://www.merriam-webster.com (1May 2020).

4. " post traumatic stress disorder." Merriam-Webster.com. 2020. https://www.merriam-webster.com (1May 2020).

5. " trauma." Merriam-Webster.com. 2020. https://www.merriam-webster.com (1May 2020).

6. " hypoxia." Merriam-Webster.com. 2020. https://www.merriam-webster.com (1May 2020).

7. " anoxia." Merriam-Webster.com. 2020. https://www.merriam-webster.com (1May 2020).

8. " perception." Merriam-Webster.com. 2020. https://www.merriam-webster.com (1May 2020).

9. " homeostasis." Merriam-Webster.com. 2020. https://www.merriam-webster.com (1May 2020).

10. " hypoxia." Merriam-Webster.com. 2020. https://www.merriam-webster.com (1May 2020).

11. " thermoception." Medical Dictionary. 2020. https://medical-dictionary.thefreedictionary.com (8 June 2020).

12. " nociception." Medical Dictionary. 2020. https://medical-dictionary.thefreedictionary.com (8 June 2020).

13. " equilibrioception." Medical Dictionary. 2020. https://medical-dictionary.thefreedictionary.com (8 June 2020).

14. " proprioception." Medical Dictionary. 2020. https://medical-dictionary.thefreedictionary.com (8 June2020).